Hip 2 Square

Square Treats
Hip Eats

Printed in the United States of America
by G&R Publishing Co.

Published By:

507 Industrial Street
Waverly, IA 50677

ISBN-13: 978-1-56383-372-4
ISBN-10: 1-56383-372-7
Item # 7049

WAYS TO SHARE A SQUARE OR TWO...

Gift giving can be fun, practical... and delicious. Before wrapping bars to give away, be sure they have cooled completely and that soft bars and crisp bars aren't packaged together. Here are a few ideas for giving bars:

- Pack bars in a heavy-duty box between layers of tissue paper or waxed paper. Replace the lid and wrap the box with pretty paper and a bow.

- Stack a few sturdy bars, wrap in plastic wrap and tie with a colorful ribbon.

- Pick up a collection of pretty plates at thrift stores. Fill them with bars, cover with colored plastic wrap and add a bow.

- Add a cloth napkin to a basket and arrange bars inside.

- Fill a tall, narrow gift bag with a tower of bars cut slightly smaller than the opening of the bag. Fill with colorful, shredded paper.

- Layer a metal loaf pan with bars and foil. Wrap with a silver ribbon.

- Make a small box from heavy decorative card stock. Place a paper doily or a square paper brownie liner in the bottom and insert one bar.

- Line the sides of a square tin with corrugated paper, using short strips to divide the tin into sections and fill each section with several bars.

- To ship bars through the mail, send only dense bar types and those that don't require refrigeration. Individually wrap each bar with plastic wrap. Place a piece of bubble wrap on the bottom of a sturdy container, then layer waxed paper between layers of bars until the container is nearly full. Crumple up tissue paper to fill any empty spaces. Cover with waxed paper and bubble wrap and seal the container.

Raspberry Chocolate Streusel Bars

Makes 16 to 25 squares

Crust & Topping ■

1½ C. flour
1½ C. quick-cooking
   or old-fashioned oats
½ C. sugar

½ C. brown sugar
1 tsp. baking powder
¼ tsp. salt
1 C. butter, softened

Filling ■

¾ C. raspberry preserves

1 (11.5 oz.) pkg. semi-sweet
  chocolate chunks

¼ C. chopped walnuts

Preparation ■

Preheat oven to 375°. Grease a 9 x 9˝ baking pan. For crust,
in a medium bowl, stir together flour, oats, sugar, brown sugar,
baking powder and salt. Cut in butter with a pastry blender
or two knives until crumbly; reserve ¾ cup mixture for topping.
Press remaining mixture into prepared pan.

For filling, spread preserves over crust and sprinkle with
chocolate chunks. In a small bowl, stir together reserved oat
mixture and walnuts; sprinkle over chocolate in pan and press
down lightly. Bake for 30 to 35 minutes or until golden brown.
Cool completely in pan until chocolate is firm, or refrigerate
for 30 minutes. Cut into squares.

Sunshine Lemon Bars

Makes 16 squares

Crust

⅓ C. butter, softened
¼ C. powdered sugar

1 C. flour

Filling

2 eggs	½ tsp. lemon flavoring
1 C. sugar	½ tsp. baking powder
2 T. flour	¼ tsp. salt
2 T. lemon juice	Additional powdered sugar

Preparation

Preheat oven to 375°. For crust, in a medium mixing bowl, cream together butter and powdered sugar with an electric mixer on medium speed until light and fluffy. Add flour; beat until crumbly. Press into an ungreased 8 x 8″ baking pan. Bake for 15 minutes.

To prepare topping, in a medium mixing bowl, combine eggs, sugar, flour, lemon juice, lemon flavoring, baking powder and salt. Beat with an electric mixer on medium speed until frothy; pour over hot crust. Bake for 18 to 22 minutes or until light golden brown. Cool in pan on a wire rack. Dust with powdered sugar. Cut into squares.

Cherry Cheesecake Squares

Makes 25 squares

Crust

2 C. graham cracker crumbs
¼ C. sugar
¼ C. butter, melted

Filling

2 (8 oz.) pkgs. cream cheese, softened
½ C. sugar
½ tsp. vanilla extract
2 eggs

8

Topping ■

1 (20 oz.) can cherry pie filling

Preparation ■

Preheat oven to 350°. For crust, in a medium bowl, mix together graham cracker crumbs, sugar and butter. Press into an ungreased 9 x 9″ baking pan. Bake for 10 minutes.

To make filling, in a large mixing bowl, beat cream cheese with an electric mixer on medium speed until smooth. Add sugar and vanilla, mixing until well blended. Add eggs, mixing until just blended. Pour over crust. Bake for 35 to 45 minutes or until center is almost set; cool. Refrigerate for 3 hours or overnight. Cut into squares. Top with pie filling before serving.

Oatmeal Caramelitas

Makes 24 to 32 squares

Crust ■

2 C. flour
2 C. quick-cooking oats
1½ C. brown sugar

1 tsp. baking soda
½ tsp. salt
1¼ C. butter, softened

Topping ■

1¼ C. semi-sweet chocolate
  chips, divided
½ C. walnuts or pecans,
  chopped

1 (12 oz.) jar caramel
  ice cream topping
3 T. flour

Preparation ■

Preheat oven to 350°. Spray a 9 x 13″ baking pan with nonstick
cooking spray; set aside. For crust, in a large bowl, combine
flour, oats, brown sugar, baking soda and salt. Cut in butter with
a pastry blender or two knives until crumbly. Set aside half the
crumb mixture; press remaining crumb mixture into prepared
pan. Bake for 10 minutes. Remove from oven.

For topping, sprinkle hot bars with 1 cup chocolate chips
and walnuts. In a small bowl, blend together caramel topping
and flour. Drizzle mixture over walnuts in pan. Sprinkle with
reserved crumbs. Return to oven and bake for 18 to 22 minutes
or until golden brown. Place pan on a wire rack to cool.
Refrigerate several hours before cutting into squares. In a small
microwave-safe bowl, melt remaining ¼ cup chocolate chips;
drizzle over cooled squares.

Spiced Pumpkin Fudge

Makes 48 to 64 squares

Fudge ▪

2 C. sugar
1 C. brown sugar
¾ C. butter
⅔ C. evaporated milk
½ C. pumpkin puree

2 tsp. pumpkin pie spice
2 C. white baking chips
1 (7 oz.) jar marshmallow creme
1 C. chopped pecans
1½ tsp. vanilla extract

Preparation

Line a 9 x 13″ baking pan with aluminum foil, extending foil beyond sides of pan. In a medium saucepan over medium heat, stir together sugar, brown sugar, butter, milk, pumpkin, and pumpkin pie spice. Stirring constantly, bring to a full, rolling boil and cook for 10 to 12 minutes or until candy thermometer reads 235° to 240° (soft-ball stage). Quickly stir in baking chips, marshmallow creme, pecans and vanilla. Stir vigorously for 1 minute or until baking chips are completely melted. Immediately pour into prepared pan; smooth top. Let stand on a wire rack for 2 hours or until completely cooled.

Cover cooled fudge tightly and refrigerate to chill. To serve, lift foil and fudge from pan. Cut fudge into small squares and remove foil.

Variation: *Try replacing the white baking chips with butterscotch chips.*

Almond Bark Bars

Makes 24 to 32 squares

Bars ■

1½ lbs. white almond bark
1 C. crunchy peanut butter
2½ C. miniature marshmallows

1 C. salted peanuts
3 C. crisp rice cereal
½ to 1 C. M&M's Mini Baking Bits

Preparation ▪

Spray a 10 x 15″ jellyroll pan with nonstick cooking spray; set aside. In the top of a double boiler, melt almond bark, stirring until melted and smooth. Stir in peanut butter until well combined. Let cool slightly.

In a large bowl, stir together marshmallows, peanuts and cereal. Pour almond bark mixture over cereal mixture. Stir until well combined. Press evenly into prepared pan. Sprinkle with baking bits, pressing down lightly. Cool before cutting into squares.

Blueberry Crumb Bars

Makes 24 squares

Crust & Topping

1 C. sugar
3 C. flour
1 tsp. baking powder
¼ tsp. salt

1 T. grated lemon peel
1 C. butter, softened
1 egg

Filling

½ C. sugar
4 tsp. cornstarch

2 T. lemon juice
4 C. fresh blueberries

Preparation

Preheat oven to 375°. Spray a 9 x 13˝ baking pan with
nonstick cooking spray; set aside. For crust, in a medium bowl,
stir together sugar, flour and baking powder. Mix in salt and
lemon peel. Cut in butter and egg with a pastry blender or two
knives until crumbly. Press half the mixture into prepared pan;
reserve remaining mixture.

To make filling, in a large bowl, stir together sugar, cornstarch
and lemon juice. Gently fold in blueberries. Spoon blueberry
mixture evenly over crust in pan. Sprinkle remaining crumb
mixture over berries. Bake for 45 minutes or until top is lightly
browned. Cool completely before cutting into squares.

Salted Peanut Chews

Makes 18 to 24 squares

Crust

1½ C. flour
⅔ C. brown sugar
½ tsp. baking powder
½ tsp. salt
¼ tsp. baking soda

½ C. butter, softened
1 tsp. vanilla extract
2 egg yolks
3 C. miniature marshmallows

Topping

⅔ C. light corn syrup
¼ C. butter
2 tsp. vanilla extract
1 (10 oz.) pkg. peanut
   butter chips

2 C. crisp rice cereal
2 C. salted peanuts

Preparation

Preheat oven to 350°. To make crust, in a large bowl, combine
flour, brown sugar, baking powder, salt, baking soda, butter,
vanilla and egg yolks. Mix well. Press evenly into an ungreased
9 x 13″ baking pan. Bake for 12 to 15 minutes or until light golden
brown. Sprinkle with marshmallows and bake 1 to 2 minutes
more until marshmallows begin to puff. Cool.

To prepare topping, in a large saucepan over medium heat,
combine syrup, butter, vanilla and peanut butter chips. Cook,
stirring constantly, until chips are melted and mixture is smooth.
Remove from heat; stir in cereal and peanuts. Immediately
spoon mixture into pan, spreading to cover marshmallows.
Cool before cutting into squares.

Blonde Brownies

Makes 24 squares

Brownies

½ C. butter
1 C. butterscotch chips
⅔ C. brown sugar
2 eggs
1 tsp. vanilla extract
1½ C. flour

2 tsp. baking powder
½ tsp. salt
2 C. miniature marshmallows
1 C. semi-sweet chocolate chips
1 C. walnuts or pecans

Preparation ■

Preheat oven to 350°. Spray a 9 x 13″ baking pan with nonstick cooking spray; set aside. In a microwave-safe bowl, combine butter and butterscotch chips. Microwave for 1 minute; stir. Microwave 1 minute more; stir until smooth. Set aside to cool. In a large bowl, stir together brown sugar, eggs and vanilla. Add cooled butterscotch mixture, flour, baking powder and salt, stirring until smooth. Stir in marshmallows, chocolate chips and walnuts. Spread in prepared pan. Bake for 15 to 20 minutes. Cool and cut into squares.

S'More Snackin' Bars

Makes 20 squares

Bars

2½ C. graham cracker crumbs
½ C. sugar
⅓ C. cake flour
⅓ C. whole wheat flour
2 tsp. baking powder

¼ tsp. salt
3 egg whites
1 C. milk
¼ C. unsweetened applesauce
¼ C. canola oil

Topping

2 C. miniature marshmallows
½ C. chopped walnuts or
   pecans, optional

1 C. milk chocolate chips

Preparation

Preheat oven to 350°. Spray a 9 x 13″ baking pan with nonstick cooking spray; set aside. For bars, in a large bowl, stir together cracker crumbs, sugar, cake flour, whole wheat flour, baking powder and salt. In a small bowl, whisk together egg whites, milk, applesauce and oil; add to dry ingredients, stirring until just moistened. Pour mixture into prepared pan. Bake for 12 to 15 minutes or until a toothpick inserted near the center comes out clean.

For topping, sprinkle hot bars with marshmallows. Return to oven and bake 3 to 4 minutes longer or until marshmallows are very soft but not brown. Remove from oven and carefully spread marshmallows with an offset spatula that has been dipped in warm water. Sprinkle with chopped walnuts, if desired. Cool on a wire rack for 10 minutes. In a microwave-safe bowl, melt chocolate chips; stir until smooth. Drizzle over bars. Cool completely on a wire rack.

Lemon Meringue Cheesecake Squares

Makes 25 squares

Bars & Meringue ■

2 (8 oz.) pkgs. cream cheese, softened

4 eggs, divided

1 C. whipping cream

1 T. self-rising flour*

½ tsp. vanilla extract

1 T. lemon juice

1 to 2 T. grated lemon peel

1 C. sugar, divided

Preparation ■

Preheat oven to 350°. Spray an 8 x 8″ baking pan with nonstick cooking spray; set aside. For bars, in a large mixing bowl, beat cream cheese with an electric mixer on medium speed until smooth. Add 1 egg, 3 egg yolks, cream, flour, vanilla, lemon juice, lemon peel and ¾ cup sugar. Mix until well combined. Pour mixture into prepared pan and bake for 20 minutes.

To make meringue, in a small, glass mixing bowl, beat 3 egg whites with an electric mixer on high speed until soft peaks form. Gradually beat in ¼ cup sugar, beating until still peaks form. Spread meringue mixture evenly on top of bars in pan, sealing at edges of pan. Return to oven and continue baking for 20 to 25 minutes. Cool before cutting into squares. Store in refrigerator.

Or substitute 1 cup all-purpose flour mixed with 1¼ teaspoons baking powder and ¼ teaspoon salt for self-rising flour. Remove 1 tablespoon for recipe and store the remainder in an air-tight container for future use.

Lime Chiffon Squares

Makes 15 to 18 squares

Crust

3 C. vanilla wafer crumbs
⅔ C. sugar

1 C. butter, melted

Filling

- 1 (3 oz.) pkg.
  lime-flavored gelatin
- 1 (8 oz.) pkg. plus 1 (3 oz.) pkg.
  cream cheese, softened
- 1 C. sugar
- 1 tsp. vanilla extract
- 1 (16 oz.) container whipped
  topping, thawed

Preparation

For crust, in a small bowl, blend together wafer crumbs, sugar and butter. Press into an ungreased 9 x 13″ baking pan; set aside.

To prepare filling, in a small bowl, dissolve gelatin in 1 cup boiling water; cool. In a large mixing bowl, beat cream cheese with an electric mixer on medium speed until smooth. Beat in sugar and vanilla until well combined. Slowly add gelatin, mixing on low speed until combined. Fold in whipped topping. Spoon mixture over crust. Refrigerate for 3 hours or until set. Garnish as desired.

Buttermilk Brownies

Makes 24 squares

Brownies

2 C. flour
2 C. sugar
1 tsp. baking soda
¼ tsp. salt
1 C. butter

⅓ C. unsweetened
  cocoa powder
2 eggs
½ C. buttermilk
1½ tsp. vanilla extract

Frosting

¼ C. butter
3 T. unsweetened cocoa
   powder

3 T. buttermilk
2¼ C. powdered sugar
½ tsp. vanilla extract

Preparation

Preheat oven to 350°. Spray a 10 x 15″ jellyroll pan with nonstick cooking spray; set aside. For brownies, in a medium bowl, stir together flour, sugar, baking soda and salt; set aside. In a medium saucepan, combine 1 cup water, butter and cocoa powder. Bring mixture just to boiling, stirring constantly. Remove from heat. Add cocoa mixture to flour mixture and beat until combined. Add eggs, one at a time, beating well after each addition. Add buttermilk and vanilla; beat for 1 minute. Pour batter into prepared pan. Bake for 25 minutes or until a toothpick inserted in the center comes out clean.

To prepare frosting, in a medium saucepan, whisk together butter, cocoa powder and buttermilk. Bring to a boil; remove from heat. Add powdered sugar and vanilla, beating with an electric mixer on medium speed until smooth. Pour warm frosting over warm brownies, spreading evenly. Cool completely in pan on a wire rack; cut into squares.

Aussie Custard Squares

Makes 9 to 12 squares

Squares

2 sheets puff pastry, thawed
1 vanilla bean*
2 C. milk
2 C. half-and-half
1 C. sugar
¾ C. cornstarch

½ C. custard powder**
3 egg yolks
1½ tsp. vanilla extract
¼ C. cubed butter
Powdered sugar

Preparation ■

Preheat oven to 400°. Line a 10 x 15″ jellyroll pan with parchment paper. Place thawed puff pastry sheets on prepared pan and bake for 15 to 18 minutes or until golden brown. Cool completely on a wire rack. Line a 9 x 9″ baking pan with aluminum foil, extending foil beyond sides of pan. Place one pastry in pan, trimming to fit, if necessary. Gently flatten.

Break vanilla bean in half and place in a medium saucepan with milk. Bring to a simmer and remove from heat. Scrape seeds from vanilla bean into milk. In a medium bowl, whisk together half-and-half, sugar, cornstarch, custard powder and egg yolks until very smooth. Whisk into milk in saucepan. Return saucepan to heat. Increase heat to medium and cook until mixture comes to a boil and is very thick, whisking frequently. Stir in vanilla and butter until butter is melted. Pour mixture over crust in pan, smoothing top. Cover mixture with remaining pastry, trimmed to fit, if necessary; gently flatten. Refrigerate 6 hours or overnight. Slice with a sharp knife, then lift foil to remove bars from pan. Remove bars from foil. Dust bars generously with powdered sugar before serving.

 * Or substitute 2 teaspoons vanilla extract for vanilla bean.

** Or substitute cook-and-serve vanilla pudding mix for custard powder.

Coconut Macaroon Swooners

Makes 24 squares

Bars

1 (10 oz.) pkg. sweetened
  flaked coconut
¾ C. sugar
¼ C. flour
¼ tsp. salt
3 egg whites at room
  temperature

1 egg, slightly beaten
1 tsp. almond extract
½ to 1 C. Hershey's Mini Kisses
  Milk Chocolate Baking Pieces

Preparation

Preheat oven to 350°. Spray 9 x 9″ baking pan with nonstick cooking spray; set aside. In a large bowl, stir together coconut, sugar, flour and salt. Mix in egg whites, egg and almond extract, stirring until well blended. Spread evenly in prepared pan. Bake for 35 minutes or until lightly browned. Remove from oven and sprinkle with chocolate baking pieces; press down lightly. Cool completely in pan on a wire rack. Cover with aluminum foil; let stand at room temperature overnight before cutting into squares.

No-Bake PB Crunch Bars

Makes 36 squares

Bars ■

1½ C. brown sugar
1¼ C. light corn syrup
1½ C. creamy peanut butter
6 C. Special K cereal

Frosting ■

½ C. creamy peanut butter
1 C. semi-sweet chocolate chips
1 C. butterscotch chips

Preparation ■

Spray a 9 x 13″ pan with nonstick cooking spray; set aside. To prepare bars, in a large, microwave-safe bowl, combine brown sugar and syrup; mix well. Cook at full power for 2 minutes. Remove from microwave and stir, scraping down sides of bowl. Microwave for an additional 2 minutes or until mixture starts to bubble around the edges. Add peanut butter; stir until smooth and well blended. Add cereal and mix until completely coated. Spread mixture in prepared pan, pressing down evenly.

For frosting, in a medium microwave-safe bowl, combine peanut butter, chocolate chips and butterscotch chips. Cook at medium power for 2 minutes; remove and stir until chips are melted, heating in 20-second intervals, if needed. Spread evenly over cereal mixture in pan. Cool to room temperature before cutting into squares.

Strawberry Rhubarb Snack Bars

Makes 15 squares

Filling

- ⅔ C. sugar
- ⅓ C. cornstarch
- 2 C. chopped fresh or frozen rhubarb
- 1 (10 oz.) pkg. frozen sweetened sliced strawberries, thawed
- 2 T. lemon juice

Bars

- 3 C. flour
- 1 C. sugar
- 1 tsp. baking powder
- ½ tsp. baking soda
- 1 C. butter
- 2 eggs
- 1 C. buttermilk
- 1 tsp. vanilla extract

Topping

¾ C. sugar   ¼ C. butter, softened
½ C. flour

Preparation

For filling, in a medium saucepan, stir together sugar and
cornstarch. Stir in rhubarb and strawberries. Bring mixture to a boil
over medium heat and cook for 2 minutes or until thickened,
stirring constantly. Remove from heat; stir in lemon juice. Cool.

Preheat oven to 350°. Spray a 9 x 13″ baking pan with nonstick
cooking spray; set aside. To make bars, in a large bowl, stir
together flour, sugar, baking powder and baking soda. Cut in
butter with a pastry blender or two knives until crumbly. In a
medium bowl, beat together eggs, buttermilk and vanilla; add
to crumb mixture, stirring just until moistened. Spoon half the
batter into prepared pan; spoon half the cooled filling over
batter. Top with remaining batter and filling.

To prepare topping, in a small bowl, stir together sugar and flour.
Cut in butter with a pastry blender or two knives until crumbly.
Sprinkle over filling in pan. Bake for 45 to 50 minutes or until a
toothpick inserted near the center comes out clean and bars are
golden brown. Cool on a wire rack before cutting into squares.

Chocolate Almond Squares

Makes 36 squares

Crust

1½ C. flour
⅔ C. sugar
¾ C. butter, softened

Bars

1 C. semi-sweet chocolate chips
1 (14 oz.) can sweetened condensed milk
1 egg, lightly beaten
2 C. almonds or walnuts, toasted and chopped
½ tsp. almond extract

Icing ■

2 tsp. shortening   2 C. semi-sweet chocolate chips

Preparation ■

Preheat oven to 350°. For crust, in a small bowl, combine flour and sugar. Cut in butter with a pastry blender or 2 knives until crumbly. Spray a 9 x 13″ baking pan with nonstick cooking spray and press crumbs into pan. Bake for 20 minutes or until lightly browned.

To make bars, in a medium saucepan over medium heat, combine chocolate chips and milk, stirring until chips are melted; cool slightly. Beat in egg. Stir in almonds and almond extract. Carefully spread over partially baked crust. Return to oven and bake an additional 25 minutes or until set; cool.

For icing, in a small saucepan over low heat, combine shortening and chocolate chips, stirring until chips are melted. Spread over bars; chill 10 minutes or until set. Cut into squares.

Crumble Bars

Makes 24 squares

Bars ■

2½ C. sifted flour, divided
2 C. brown sugar
½ C. butter, softened
1 egg, beaten

2 tsp. baking powder
1 tsp. ground cinnamon
¾ C. milk

40

Preparation ■

Preheat oven to 350°. Spray a 9 x 13″ baking pan with nonstick cooking spray; set aside. In a large bowl, combine 2 cups flour and brown sugar; Cut in butter with a pastry blender or two knives until crumbly. Set aside ½ cup crumb mixture.

To crumb mixture still in bowl, add egg, remaining ½ cup flour, baking powder, cinnamon and milk. Blend with an electric mixer on low speed until well combined. Spread batter evenly in prepared pan. Sprinkle reserved crumbs over batter and bake for 35 to 40 minutes or until a toothpick inserted in the center comes out clean. Cool before cutting into squares.

Banana Crunch
Squares

Makes 16 to 20 squares

Crust ■

1¾ C. crushed chocolate
   wafers (about 36)
½ C. sugar
¼ C. unsweetened
   cocoa powder
1 tsp. vanilla extract
½ C. butter, melted

Filling ■

3 T. light corn syrup
2 T. butter
2 medium bananas, sliced
1 tsp. rum flavoring

Icing

½ C. semi-sweet
 chocolate chips

½ C. peanut butter chips
1 tsp. shortening

Preparation

Preheat oven to 350°. Spray an 8 x 8″ baking pan with
nonstick cooking spray; set aside. For crust, in a medium bowl,
stir together wafer crumbs, sugar, cocoa powder and vanilla;
stir in melted butter. Press mixture evenly into prepared pan.
Bake for 10 minutes. Cool for 10 minutes in pan on a wire rack.

To prepare filling, in a small saucepan over medium heat,
combine syrup and butter. Stir until melted and bubbly.
Remove from heat; stir in bananas and rum flavoring. Spoon
banana mixture evenly over baked crust.

For icing, in a small saucepan over low heat, combine
chocolate chips, peanut butter chips and shortening. Cook
and stir until chips are completely melted. Drizzle mixture over
banana mixture in pan. Cover and chill in refrigerator until set.
Remove from refrigerator and let stand at room temperature
for 20 minutes before cutting into squares. Serve immediately.

Chocolate Mint Brownies

Makes 16 squares

Brownies ■

½ C. butter
4 oz. unsweetened baking
   chocolate
1½ C. sugar

3 eggs
1½ tsp. vanilla extract
1 C. flour
½ tsp. salt

Frosting & Icing ■

¼ C. butter, softened
2½ C. powdered sugar
1½ to 3 T. milk
½ tsp. peppermint extract

Green food coloring
¾ C. milk chocolate chips
1 tsp. butter

Preparation ■

Preheat oven to 350°. Spray a 9 x 9″ baking pan with nonstick cooking spray; set aside. For brownies, in a small microwave-safe bowl, melt butter and baking chocolate, stirring occasionally. In a large bowl, whisk together sugar and eggs. Stir in chocolate mixture, vanilla, flour and salt until thoroughly combined. Pour into prepared pan; bake for 25 minutes or until a toothpick inserted in the center comes out clean. Cool.

For frosting, in a medium mixing bowl, beat together butter and powdered sugar with an electric mixer on medium speed until smooth and creamy. Add milk, 1 tablespoon at a time, beating until spreadable. Stir in peppermint extract and food coloring. Spread on cooled brownies; chill for 1 hour. For icing, in a small microwave-safe bowl, melt chocolate chips and butter; stir until smooth. Drizzle over brownies; chill for 1 hour. Bring to room temperature and cut into squares.

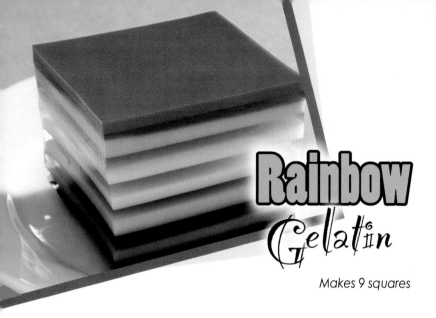

Rainbow Gelatin

Makes 9 squares

Gelatin ■

1 (3 oz.) pkg. grape-
flavored gelatin

1 (3 oz.) pkg. blueberry-
flavored gelatin

1 (3 oz.) pkg. lime-
flavored gelatin

1 (3 oz.) pkg. lemon-
flavored gelatin

1 (3 oz.) pkg. orange-
flavored gelatin

1 (3 oz.) pkg. cherry-
flavored gelatin

1 C. plus 2 T. sour cream or
vanilla yogurt, divided

Preparation ■

Spray an 8 x 8″ or a 9 x 9″ pan with nonstick cooking spray; set aside. In a small bowl, combine grape-flavored gelatin and 1¼ cups boiling water. Whisk at least 2 minutes until completely dissolved. Pour ¾ cup gelatin mixture into prepared pan. Refrigerate 15 to 30 minutes or until set but not firm (gelatin should stick to finger when touched). Refrigerate remaining gelatin in bowl 5 to 10 minutes or until slightly thickened (the consistency of unbeaten egg whites). Gradually whisk 3 tablespoons sour cream into gelatin remaining in bowl. Spoon over gelatin in pan. Refrigerate 15 to 30 minutes or until gelatin is set but not firm.

Repeat the process with each remaining gelatin flavor to create 12 alternating clear and creamy gelatin layers. Refrigerate for 2 hours or until firm. Cut into squares and carefully remove from pan with a thin metal spatula.

Graham Cracker *Snackers*

Makes 24 squares

Bars ■

¾ C. butter
¾ C. sugar
¼ C. milk
1 egg, slightly beaten
1 C. chopped pecans, toasted
1 C. graham cracker crumbs
12 graham cracker rectangles

Frosting ■

½ C. brown sugar
1 oz. semi-sweet
   baking chocolate
3 T. butter
1 tsp. vanilla
2 C. powdered sugar

Icing ■

½ C. powdered sugar   2 to 3 tsp. milk

Preparation ■

To make bars, in a medium saucepan over medium heat, combine butter, sugar, milk and egg. Stir constantly until mixture comes to a full boil. Remove from heat. Stir in pecans and cracker crumbs. Cool slightly. Meanwhile, line a 7 x 11″ baking pan with six graham cracker rectangles. Cover with pecan mixture; spread evenly. Place remaining cracker rectangles on top, matching them up with bottom crackers.

For frosting, in a medium saucepan over medium heat, bring brown sugar, baking chocolate and 2 tablespoons water to a boil. Remove from heat and stir in butter and vanilla. Beat in powdered sugar until well combined. Frost bars. Refrigerate overnight and cut into squares.

For icing, in a small bowl, whisk together powdered sugar and enough milk to make a drizzling consistency. Drizzle over frosted bars.

Tropical Fruit *Gems*

Makes 72 squares

Bars ■

- 1 (16.5 oz.) pkg. refrigerated
  sugar cookie dough
- 1 (14 oz.) can sweetened
  condensed milk
- 1 (6 oz.) pkg. dried pineapple,
  chopped (about 1½ C.)

- 1 C. semi-sweet
  chocolate chips
- 1⅓ C. sweetened
  flaked coconut
- ⅔ C. cashew halves

Preparation ■

Preheat oven to 350°. Spray a 10 x 15″ jellyroll pan with nonstick cooking spray. With floured hands, press cookie dough evenly into bottom of prepared pan. Pour milk evenly over dough. Sprinkle with pineapple, chocolate chips, coconut and cashews. Press down firmly. Bake for 20 to 30 minutes or until lightly browned. Cool in pan on a wire rack and cut into squares.

Nanaimo Bars

Makes 16 squares

Crust

½ C. butter

¼ C. sugar

5 T. unsweetened
cocoa powder, sifted

1 egg

1 tsp. vanilla extract

1½ C. chocolate wafer crumbs

1 C. sweetened
flaked coconut

½ C. chopped walnuts, toasted

Filling

⅓ C. butter, softened
1½ T. vanilla instant pudding mix
¼ C. milk

2 tsp. vanilla extract
3 C. powdered sugar, sifted

Frosting

8 oz. semi-sweet baking
  chocolate, chopped

2 T. butter

Preparation

Preheat oven to 350°. Spray an 8 x 8˝ baking pan with nonstick cooking spray; set aside. For crust, in a medium saucepan over medium heat, melt butter. Stir in sugar and cocoa powder; blend well. In a small bowl, whisk together egg and vanilla; add to hot mixture. Stir in wafer crumbs, coconut and walnuts; press into prepared pan and bake for 10 minutes. Chill.

To prepare filling, in a large bowl, beat butter and pudding mix until smooth. Stir in milk, vanilla and powdered sugar, 1 cup at a time, until well combined. Carefully spread over crust; chill.

For frosting, in the top of a double boiler over medium heat, combine chocolate and butter, stirring until melted and smooth. Spread evenly over filling in pan. Chill for 30 minutes.

Cherry Nut Squares

Makes 24 to 32 squares

Bars ■

½ C. brown sugar
½ C. sugar
½ C. shortening
2 eggs
1 tsp. vanilla extract
¼ tsp. coconut flavoring

2 C. flour
1½ tsp. baking powder
¾ C. milk
1 C. chopped walnuts
1 C. maraschino cherry halves, drained, juice reserved

Icing ■

2 C. powdered sugar, sifted   Vegetable oil
3 T. milk or reserved cherry juice

Preparation ■

Preheat oven to 325°. Spray a 10 x 15″ jellyroll pan with
nonstick cooking spray; set aside. To make bars, in a large
mixing bowl, beat together brown sugar, sugar and shortening
with an electric mixer on medium speed until creamy. Add
eggs, vanilla, coconut flavoring, flour, baking powder, milk and
walnuts. Blend until well combined. Fold in cherries. Spread
evenly in prepared pan. Bake for 25 to 30 minutes.

To make icing, in a medium bowl, combine powdered sugar,
milk and about 3 drops of oil; mix until smooth. Drizzle over
warm bars.

Peanut Butter Bars

Makes 16 squares

Crust ■

6 T. butter
¼ C. sugar
1½ C. graham cracker crumbs

Filling ■

½ C. butter
1¾ C. powdered sugar
1 C. creamy peanut butter

56

Frosting ■

¼ C. butter

½ C. semi-sweet
chocolate chips

Preparation ■

Line an 8 x 8″ baking pan with aluminum foil, extending foil beyond sides of pan. For crust, in a small, microwave-safe bowl, melt butter. Stir in sugar and cracker crumbs until well combined. Press firmly into prepared pan; set aside.

To prepare filling, in a medium saucepan over medium heat, melt butter. Remove from heat and beat in powdered sugar with an electric mixer on medium speed until smooth. Add peanut butter, mixing until creamy. Pour mixture evenly over crust in pan.

For frosting, in a small saucepan over low heat, melt butter. Add chocolate chips and stir until chips are nearly melted and very soft. Remove from heat and continue stirring until chocolate is smooth and shiny. Pour evenly over peanut butter layer. Refrigerate for 30 minutes. Lift foil and bars from pan; cut into squares and remove foil. Store in the refrigerator.

Extreme Crispy Bars

Makes 15 to 18 squares

Bars ▪

2 (10.5 oz.) bags miniature marshmallows
6 to 7 T. butter
12 C. crisp rice cereal

Topping ▪

1 C. miniature semi-sweet chocolate chips
3 C. miniature marshmallows
10 miniature Twix candy bars, chopped
10 miniature Snickers candy bars, chopped

58

Preparation ■

Preheat oven to broil, moving oven rack to middle position. Spray a 9 x 13″ pan with nonstick cooking spray; set aside. To make bars, in a very large saucepan over medium heat, melt marshmallows and butter, stirring constantly until marshmallows are melted. Stir in cereal until well coated. Press into prepared pan.

Sprinkle chocolate chips over cereal mixture in pan, then sprinkle with marshmallows. Broil 30 to 60 seconds, just until marshmallows start to puff and turn golden brown. Remove from oven and press chopped candy bars over toasted marshmallows. Cut into squares.

Metric Conversion Chart

Abbreviations

C. = cup	qt. = quart	mL = milliliter
T. = tablespoon	gal. = gallon	F = Fahrenheit
tsp. = teaspoon	lb. = pound	C = Celsius
oz. = ounce	g = gram	
pt. = pint	L = liter	

Weights (mass)

½ oz.	15 g
1 oz.	30 g
3 oz.	90 g
4 oz.	120 g
8 oz.	225 g
10 oz.	285 g
12 oz.	360 g
16 oz. (1 lb.)	450 g

Oven Temperatures

250°F	120°C
275°F	140°C
300°F	150°C
325°F	160°C
350°F	180°C
375°F	190°C
400°F	200°C
425°F	220°C
450°F	230°C

Baking Pan Sizes

Pan Size	Size (in/ qt)	Metric Volume	Size (cm)
Baking or Cake Pan (square or rectangle)	8 x 8 x 2	2 L	20 x 20 x 5
	9 x 9 x 2	2.5 L	23 x 23 x 5
	8 x 12 x 2	3 L	30 x 20 x 5
	9 x 13 x 2	3.5 L	33 x 23 x 5
Loaf Pan	4 x 8 x 3	1.5 L	20 x 10 x 7
	5 x 9 x 3	2 L	23 x 13 x 7
Round Layer Cake Pan	8 x 1½	1.2 L	20 x 4
	9 x 1½	1.5 L	23 x 4
Pie Plate	8 x 1¼	750 mL	20 x 3
	9 x 1¼	1 L	23 x 3
Baking Dish or Casserole	1 quart	1 L	–
	1½ quart	1.5 L	–
	2 quart	2 L	–

Volume Measurements (dry)

⅛ tsp.	0.5 mL
¼ tsp.	1 mL
½ tsp.	2 mL
¾ tsp.	4 mL
1 tsp.	5 mL
1 T.	15 mL
2 T.	30 mL
¼ C.	60 mL
⅓ C.	75 mL
½ C.	125 mL
¾ C.	175 mL
1 C.	250 mL
2 C. (1 pt.)	500 mL
3 C.	750 mL
4 C. (1 qt.)	1 L

Volume Measurements (fluid)

1 fluid oz. (2 T.)	30 mL
4 fluid oz. (½ C.)	125 mL
8 fluid oz. (1 C.)	250 mL
12 fluid oz. (1½ C.)	375 mL
16 fluid oz. (2 C.)	500 mL

Dimensions

¹⁄₁₆ inch	2 mm
⅛ inch	3 mm
¼ inch	6 mm
½ inch	1.5 cm
¾ inch	2 cm
1 inch	2.5 cm